JON GEORGE
A day in the JUNGLE

Music and Illustrations:
Jon George

Cover Design:
Jorge Paredes

© 1968 by Summy-Birchard Music
division of Summy-Birchard Inc.
All rights reserved   Printed in U.S.A.

ISBN 0-87487-630-3

Summy-Birchard Inc.
exclusively distributed by
Warner Bros. Publications
15800 N.W. 48th Avenue, Miami, Florida 33014
All rights reserved   Printed in U.S.A.

Preface

The twelve pieces in this set offer the young student a variety of intriguing pianistic experiences. Careful study of this music will contribute to development of sensitivity and to awareness of keyboard resources. Titles, illustrations, and "lyrics" are all designed to stimulate the child's imagination and encourage him to express himself vividly at the keyboard. Teaching features of each piece are listed in the Contents.

The pieces may be performed separately or in suites of various combinations of the student's choice.

Jon George

Contents

ELEPHANT WALKING

Very heavily indeed

I wonder what's happening in the jungle today.

GAZELLE PRANCING

Gaily

a very graceful creature,

full of the joy of living!

SNAKE SNEAKING

All slithery

p Sneak... sneer...

What a sneaky, sneery snake!

pp

Ouch!

NATIVES DANCING

JUNGLE RIVER FLOWING

Mysteriously

mf winding thru the jungle,

una corda

p

mp wide and deep . . .

p

mf Don't disturb the crocodile!

mp

ri -

- tar - dan - do

pp

CROCODILE BASKING

BEETLE CREEPING

(R.H. always an octave higher than written)

Steadily

mp

p

sempre legato

He's a good little fellow, really—

mp

quite harmless, as you can see...

pp

...see?

TIGER STALKING

With an evil glint in your eye

ORCHID BLOOMING

Delicately

mf
It is pale blue and very beautiful.

p *legato*

mp
Do not pick it! It should be let alone to blossom.

p *simile*

L.H.
rit. *pp*

BABOONS TALKING

With a sense of humor

mf   "Hi! What's new?"   "Grumpf!"

(L.H. always an octave lower than written)

"Grumpf!"

f "Tag, you're it!"

GIANT VINES GROWING

What a beautiful shade of green!

Its huge green leaves are shimmering in the sun!

JUNGLE SUNSET GLOWING

Warmly

(Pedal stays down throughout the piece)

So very colorful!

R.H.

L.H.

R.H.

L.H.

R.H.

L.H.

So very peaceful...